日本人のしぐさ

70 Japanese Gestures
No Language Communication

日英対訳

ハミル・アキ＝著 Hamiru・aqui

IBCパブリッシング

Preface

Japanese is considered to be an extremely difficult language to learn. The writing system is made up of over 100 phonetic symbols in addition to thousands of Chinese characters. It is often said that it takes till the age of 10 for a Japanese child to master the language.

Many people are of the belief that Japanese keep body action to a minimum when speaking, yet over 120 gestures are commonly used. Even after eliminating those that will likely disappear with the next change of generations, 70 still remain. These are presented in this book.

It is an unfortunate fact that, at present, there are many Japanese who are not proficient in English. Communicating with words may be difficult but why not start with gestures? Great insight into the culture and lifestyle of Japan can be had from understanding its gestures.

Many gestures have been influenced by the West and introduced through foreign movies. However, there still are many interesting gestures considered unique to Japan.

This book presents a mix of popular gestures, slang gestures, and gestures used by children. They range from the serious to the downright hilarious.

Also, we recommend that you watch Japanese *manga* and movies in order to better your understanding. In comic strips, animated films and old films by *Kurosawa* and *Yasujiro Ozu*, emotions and meanings not conveyed through words or facial expression are very often expressed with gestures. The reader will be able to recognize many of these after reading this book.

Armed with an understanding of many new expressions, readers will be sure to enjoy a great deal more of the Japanese and the Japanese language.

Hamiru • aqui

前書き

　日本語は、習得がとても難しい言語だと考えられています。書き言葉には、ひらがなやカタカナといった表音文字だけで100以上、さらに数千の漢字があります。日本の子どもが母国語を身につけるのに10歳までかかるという指摘もよく耳にします。

　日本人は話すときに体の動きを最小限にとどめると信じている人は多いですが、実際には、120を超えるジェスチャーが使われています。次の次の世代になるころには使わなくなりそうなものを除いても、70のジェスチャーが残ります。本書では、この70のジェスチャーを取り上げました。

　残念ながら、英語をうまく話せない日本人が多いのは事実です。言葉でのコミュニケーションは難しいかもしれませんが、ジェスチャーから始めたらどうでしょう。ジェスチャーがわかれば、日本の文化やライフスタイルがどんどん見えてくるはずです。

　欧米の影響を受けて、外国の映画を通じて入ってきたジェスチャーも数多くありますが、日本特有と考えられる、おもしろいジェスチャーもたくさんあります。

　本書では、おもしろいジェスチャー、スラング・ジェスチャー、子どもの使うジェスチャーを紹介します。まじめなものから、大笑いするものまで、いろいろなものがあります。

　また、理解を深めるために、日本のマンガや映画を見ることをおすすめします。マンガやアニメ映画、黒澤や小津安二郎の古い映画では、人の気持ちや真意をジェスチャーで表すことがよく見受けられます。本書を読めば、こうした作品に出てくるジェスチャーの多くがわかるようになるでしょう。

　多くの新しい表現を覚えれば、みなさんはきっと、日本や日本語をもっと楽しめるようになるでしょう。

ハミル・アキ

カバーデザイン = 岩目地英樹 (コムデザイン)
本文デザイン = Morisato Tomura
日本語翻訳 = 平 湊 音
英文リライト = アイリーン・チャング
Model = Takafumi Hamada

本書の英文テキストは、弊社から刊行された『Japanese 70 Gestures』と共通です。

CONTENTS

General Gestures 7
一般的なジェスチャー

Slang Gestures 63
スラング・ジェスチャー

Children's Gestures 111
子どものジェスチャー

Index 157

General Gestures
一般的なジェスチャー

The following are gestures used in daily life and are popular with both adults and children.

日常生活で大人も子どももよく使う
一般的なジェスチャーです。

01 | Bowing
おじぎ
Ojigi

Lower your head.

A movement when greeting someone.

This is a practice that is not seen in Western countries, though it is very often observed in Japan. It is believed to have its roots in China where it indicates a degree of respect or gratitude to another person. Though Japan does not have the custom of shaking hands, bowing can be looked upon as similar to the Western handshake. It seems that, in general, people bow more politely when bidding goodbye than when meeting someone. When bidding goodbye to an older person or higher-ranked person, to wait with your head bowed until the person turns his/her back, or until the door closes, is a form of showing respect to that person.

....

頭を下げる。

人にあいさつするときの動作。

日本ではとてもよく目にするが、欧米文化には見られない習慣である。おじぎのルーツは中国にあると考えられている。中国では、おじぎは相手への一定の敬意や感謝の気持ちを示す。日本には握手の習慣はないが、おじぎが欧米の握手と似たようなものと考えられている。一般に、誰かに会う時よりも、別れのあいさつをするときのほうが、おじぎをていねいにするようだ。年上の人や目上の人におじぎをするときは、相手が背中を向けたり、扉が閉まったりするまで、頭を下げたままで待っているのが、その人への敬意を示す方法である。

02 | Yes. No.
はい。 いいえ。
Hai. *Iie.*

Yes. No.

As in the West, in Japan, one nods when saying "yes" and shakes the head sideways when saying "no."

However, depending on the question, there are times when the English "yes" and "no" seem to be interchanged.

i.e.) "Aren't you going?"
　　—"Yes" (nodding the head) = ("Yes, I am not going.")

In the West this question would be answered with a "No" and a shake of the head, "No, I'm not going."

. . . .

　日本では、欧米とおなじように、「はい」というときはうなずき、「いいえ」というときは首を横に振る。

　しかし、質問のしかたによっては、英語のyes、noと「はい」、「いいえ」が逆になる。

　たとえば、
「行かないの？」
「はい。」（うなずく）＝（「はい、行かない。」）

　欧米では、こう聞かれたら「いいえ」と言って、首を横に振る。
「いいえ、行かない」

03 | Thank you.　　It was delicious!
いただきます。　　ごちそうさま。
Itadakimasu.　　*Gochisosama.*

Place both palms together and lightly bow your head.

Itadakimasu is said before eating a meal.

Make sure your chopsticks are still on the chopstick rest.

Gochisosama is said after eating a meal.

Both phrases are said while you lightly bow your head.

....

両手の手のひらを合わせて、軽く頭を下げる。

食事を始める前に、「いただきます」と言う。

はしをはし置きに置いたままにしておこう。

食事が終わったら「ごちそうさま」と言う。

両方とも、頭を軽く下げて言う言葉だ。

04 | Me
私
Watashi

Put your index finger on the tip of your nose.

In Western countries, people point to their chests when indicating themselves, but in Japan, people point to their noses. When indicating others or other things one points with the index finger to the center of the object or the person being indicated. When indicating the person one is talking to directly, the index finger is pointed at his or her nose to indicate "you." The gesture may offend a Westerner, but to the Japanese, it is not considered rude at all. For young people these days, pointing to the nose has become an outdated gesture, and, influenced by movies, they have started pointing to their chests. Nonetheless, pointing to the person one is talking to is still a common Japanese gesture.

....

　人さしゆびを鼻先に置く。

　欧米の文化では、自分のことを言う時に胸をさすが、日本では、鼻をさす。他の人やものをさすときは、人さしゆびをさしたいものや人の真ん中に向ける。話している相手をさすときは、「あなた」のことだと示すために相手の鼻に人さしゆびを向ける。このジェスチャーを見ると、欧米人は怒ることもあるが、日本人にとっては、まったく失礼なことではない。今日の若者にとっては、鼻をさすのは古いジェスチャーとなっており、映画の影響もあって、若者たちは自分の胸をさすようになっている。しかし、話をしている相手をさすジェスチャーは、日本ではいまでもよく見られる。

05 | Come over here!
こっちにおいで！
Kocchi ni oide!

Go away!
あっちいけ！
Acchi ike!

Come over here!
With the back of your hand facing upward, shake your hand downward towards yourself. Some people use both hands to gesture to a child.

Go away!
With the back of the hand facing upwards, shake your hand as if trying to shake something off.

Sometimes, the "come over here" gesture may be misunderstood as "go away." The two can be difficult to distinguish, but a nodding of the head, and the fact the person is looking at you and laughing, will make it likely that "come here" is meant. A person saying "go away" will often not make eye contact.

....

「こっちにおいで！」
　手の甲を上にして、手を自分の方に向けて下に振る。子どもに向かってジェスチャーするときには、両手を使う人もいる。

「あっちいけ！」
　手の甲を上にして、何かを払いのけるように手を振る。

　「こっちにおいで！」のジェスチャーが「あっちいけ！」と誤解されることもある。両者は区別しにくいこともあるが、うなずいていたり、相手があなたを見て笑いかけていたりしたら、たぶん「こっちにおいで！」のつもりだろう。「あっちいけ！」のジェスチャーをする人は、アイ・コンタクトを取らないことが多い。

06 | Calm down.
落ち着いて。
Ochi tsui te.

Move both hands up and down while saying "*maa maa maa*" with your palms facing the ground.

This conveys that one wants a person to calm down, cool his temper, or not be so frantic.

Maa maa maa must be said together with the hand motion. If not, people will not understand what you are trying to say. It may be best to remember the *maa maa maa* and the hand motion as one set.

・・

　「まあまあまあ」と言いながら、手のひらを地面に向けて両手を上げ下げする。

　このジェスチャーは、相手を落ち着かせて気持ちをしずめてほしい、あるいは、そんなに取り乱さないでほしいというメッセージを伝える。

　手の動きといっしょに、「まあまあまあ」と言わなければならない。そうしなければ、相手はあなたが伝えたいメッセージがなにかピンと来ないだろう。手の動きと「まあまあまあ」を一つのセットとして覚えるのがいちばんよい。

07 | I'm going to pass in front of you.
前を通ります。
Mae wo tori masu.

Round the back slightly, place one hand up with your fingers together and the thumb up, then gently move your hand up and down when passing in front of someone.

It is basically considered impolite to directly pass in front of someone. This gesture can be taken as an apology when passing in front of someone and obstructing his view, for example, in a store aisle. In Western culture, this gesture is very similar to saying "excuse me" when passing in front of someone.

You will make a positive and favorable impression with this gesture and may find people striking up a conversation with you.

....

　人の前を通るときは、背中を少し丸め、指をそろえて親ゆびが上になるようにして手を上げ、その手をゆっくり上下する。

　基本的に、人のすぐ前を通るのは、礼儀に反すると考えられている。このジェスチャーは、たとえば店の通路などで、相手の前を通って視界をさえぎることへの謝罪と受け取ることができる。欧米の文化では、人の前を通るときに「エクスキューズ・ミー」と言うが、このジェスチャーはそれにとても近い。

　このジェスチャーを用いることで、ポジティブでよい印象を与えることができる。周りの人たちがあなたに話しかけてくるかもしれない。

08 | I don't know.　　That's wrong.

知らない。　　違う。
Shiranai.　　*Chigau.*

Shake your upright hand near your mouth with your thumb closer to your face.

There are times when the head is shaken at the same time. In that case, the head and hand will move in opposite directions. When this gesture is seen, for example, when asking directions, it simply means the person does not understand English or he is unable to assist you. One is advised to simply go and ask another person.

....

　手を口の近くに持ち上げ、親ゆび側を顔に近づけて手を振る。

　同時に頭を横に振ることもある。その場合、手と頭は反対側に動く。たとえば道をたずねたときにこのジェスチャーをされたら、その人は英語がわからないか、道を教えてあげられないという意味だ。その人のもとを去って、別の人に聞くことをおすすめする。

09 | Thank you.
かたじけない。
Katajikenai.

With your thumb facing towards your face, move your hand upright to a point in front of your face.

It is the same gesture made by a *sumo* wrestler who has won as he accepts his prize money.

It is an expression derived from the handheld sword. Often it is used by men as an abbreviated form of expressing appreciation.

In Japan, there is a custom to pour drinks for one's guests. When the host sees his guest's glass is nearly empty, he will come over to refill it. Then, the guest will make this gesture to show appreciation instead of saying "thank you" in words.

....

　親ゆびを顔の方に向けて、手を顔の前まで上げる。

　相撲の力士が勝って賞金を受け取るジェスチャーとまったく同じである。

　小刀に由来する表現で、感謝の気持ちを表すときの略式の表現として、男性がよく用いる。

　日本では、客人に飲み物を注ぐ習慣がある。客人のコップが空きそうなのを主人が見て取ると、近づいて飲み物を注ぐ。そのとき、「ありがとう」と言葉に出すかわりに、客人はこのジェスチャーをして感謝の気持ちを表す。

10 | Do you want to go eat?
食事
Shokuji

Pretend to hold a rice bowl in one hand and bring a chopstick to your mouth with the other hand. Repeat the hand motion of bringing a chopstick to your mouth several times. Sometimes, only the chopstick motion is used with two fingers acting as a chopstick.

When you see someone looking at you and making this gesture, he is asking if you have already eaten or would like to go eat together. Japan is the only country in Asia where spoons are not often used for eating. The Japanese custom is to eat with a rice bowl and chopstick. Of course when Western dishes are eaten, Japanese will use a fork and spoon. At a formal Japanese dinner, chopsticks only are used. For your additional information, it is not considered impolite to drink soup directly from the bowl. You should also remember to always hold the rice bowl by supporting it with one hand underneath it.

....

　片手に茶碗を持ち、もう片方の手で箸を口に持っていく動作をまねる。箸を口に近づける動作を何度か繰り返す。二本の指を箸に見立てて、箸の動きだけをすることもある。

　相手があなたの方を見てこのジェスチャーをしたら、もう食事を済ませたか、それとも一緒に食事に行きたいかをたずねている。日本は、アジアの国の中で唯一、食事のときにスプーンをあまり使わない国だ。茶碗と箸で食事をするのが日本の慣わしである。もちろん、西洋料理を食べるときは、日本人もフォークとスプーンを使う。正式な和食では、箸だけが使われる。参考までに、スープをお椀から直接飲むのは失礼には当たらない。また、茶碗の下にいつも片手を添えて持つことを覚えておこう。

11 | Wait a moment.
ちょっと待って。
Chotto matte.

Show the palm of one hand to the other person. It also means to wait there. Both hands are used at times.

In the West, gestures meaning "wait" often involve raising your index finger. However, in Japan, showing the palm of one hand or both palms to the other person is the basic gesture. If the Western-style gesture for "wait" is made in Japan, the Japanese would think of it as "1," as in No. 1.

If a child grabs your finger when you point it upward to signify the Western "wait," you will now be aware that it's because he thinks you are starting a game.

Refer to **55** | Grab this finger! on p.**122**

....

　片手の手のひらを相手に向ける。「そこで待っていて」という意味になることもある。両手を使うこともある。

　欧米では、人さしゆびを上げるジェスチャーが「待って」という意味になることが多い。しかし日本では、相手に片手や両手の手のひらを見せるジェスチャーが基本となる。欧米式の「待って」というジェスチャーをすると、日本人は、「一番」という意味の「1」を連想するだろう。

　欧米式に「待って」というつもりで指を上に上げると、子どもがその指をつかむことがある。これは、遊びを始めようとしているとその子が思ったからだ。

12 | Formal　　Indian-style
正座　　あぐら
Seiza　　*Agura*

Formal (*Seiza*)

Indian-style (*Agura*)

The proper way to sit in a *tatami* room is in the *seiza* position, which is sitting on your knees with your legs tucked under you. In a formal setting, you would continue sitting in the *seiza* position. But once the greetings have been made and the atmosphere becomes relaxed, you may unfold and cross your legs, in the seating position Japanese call "*agura*." The host may sometimes say, "Please put yourself at ease." In which case, you would thank him before assuming the Indian-style position.

・・

　畳の敷かれた部屋での正式な座り方は正座である。脚を体の下で折り曲げて、膝を地面につけて座る。改まった場では、ずっと正座を続ける。しかし、あいさつが終わって和やかな雰囲気になったら、脚をくずして交差させ、日本語で「あぐら」という座り方に変えてもよい。主人が「どうぞ楽になさってください」と言うこともある。その場合、あぐらにする前に「ありがとうございます」と言う。

Formal (*Seiza*)

Indian-style (*Agura*)

Agura was considered a man's seating position from the time when the Japanese dressed mainly in *kimono*. Sitting in the *agura* position was considered bad manners for women. Unless in the company of close friends, it may be better for women to sit with legs unfolded, but to one side. Sitting in the *seiza* position for hours is painful even for many Japanese. The legs fall asleep and you may not be able to stand without help. There are various ways to survive long hours of *seiza* sitting. The most popular one is to cross your toes. Ask a Japanese friend for tips. You will be surprised to find out how many different ways there are.

....

あぐらは、日本人が主に着物を着ていた時代には、男性の座り方だと考えられていた。女性があぐら座りをするのはマナーが悪いと考えられていた。親しい友人と一緒にいる場合は別だが、女性は脚を片方にくずして座るほうがよい。何時間も正座で座り続けるのは、日本人でさえたいていは苦痛である。脚がしびれてしまい、助けてもらわないと立ち上がれないかもしれない。何時間も正座で座り続ける方法はいくつかある。一番よく使われているのは、足の指を重ねる方法だ。日本の友人にコツを聞いてみるとよい。いろいろと違った方法があることに驚くだろう。

13 | Tapping the shoulder
肩を叩く
Kata wo tataku

When you want to let someone know he has dropped something, or you want him to notice that you want to talk to him, or when you're meeting someone and approaching him from behind, tap the person on his shoulder two or three times to make him aware of your presence or to request his attention. The same thing is done when you want to point something out to him, for example, "Look over there!" You would tap the person on his shoulder before saying what you have to say.

Here is a joke that was once popular. You tap a person's shoulder with your index finger pointing towards his cheek; he turns his face towards you. As he does so your finger touches his cheeks. "Ouch!" he says, and you both chuckle over it.

・・・・・・・・・・・・・・・・・・・・・・・・・・・・・

　ものを落としたと知らせたいとき、話をしたいと伝えたいとき、人に会って背後から近づくとき、あなたがいることを知らせ、注意を引きたいことを知らせるために、肩を2、3回軽くたたく。たとえば、「あれを見て」というように、何かを指さすときにも、同じことをする。言いたいことを言う前に、相手の肩をたたく。

　昔流行ったジョークがある。人さしゆびを相手のほほに向けて、その人の肩をたたく。相手があなたのほうを振り向くと、あなたの人さしゆびがその人のほほに触れる。相手は「イタッ」と言い、二人でクスッと笑う。

14 | Hot!
熱い！
Atsui!

When having touched something hot like a pot, grab the earlobe with the thumb and index finger.

This comes from the fact that the earlobe has the lowest body temperature compared to other body parts. Please don't think of this gesture as meaning someone has lost a pair of earrings.

・・・・・・・・・・・・・・・・・・・・・・・・・・・・・

　なべのような熱いものに触ったとき、親ゆびと人さしゆびで耳たぶをつかむ。

　これは、耳たぶが、体のほかの部分より体温が低いことに由来する。イヤリングをなくした、というジェスチャーだと思わないように。

15 | To laugh
笑う
Warau

Covering the mouth when laughing.

In the old days in Japan, for a man to show his teeth indicated weakness or that he was joking. To show one's teeth when laughing was considered bad manners. There used to be a custom where married women painted their teeth black (*ohaguro*). To have white teeth forever meant that the woman had missed her chance to marry. Japanese hide their mouths when laughing because of this custom. However, in present-day Japan, there are many who do this in order to hide poor tooth alignment or because they feel embarrassed about something.

・・・・・・・・・・・・・・・・・・・・・・・・・・・・

笑うときは、口元を手でおおう。

昔の日本では、男性が歯を見せることは、弱さや、冗談を言っていることを意味した。笑うときに歯を見せるのは、行儀が悪いと考えられていた。昔は、既婚の女性が歯を黒く塗る習慣（お歯黒）があった。ずっと白い歯のままでいることは、女性が婚期を逃したということであった。この慣わしに由来して、日本人は笑うときに口元を隠す。しかし、今日の日本では、歯並びの悪さを隠したり、なにか決まりの悪い思いをしたりするときに、口元をおおう人も多い。

16 | Let's put that subject aside.
その話はおいといて。
Sono hanashi wa oitoi te.

The gesture looks like one is moving a box from in front of one's self to the side.

It is a gesture used when changing the subject or saying, "Let's put that subject aside and change the topic."

　このジェスチャーは、自分の目の前にある箱を横に動かすような動作をする。

　話題を変えて、「その話は置いておいて、違う話をしよう」というときに使われるジェスチャーである。

17 | I agree!
納得！
Nattoku!

Hit the palm of one hand with a closed fist.

This gesture can also be done by hitting your thighs. In that case, be sure to slap your thighs hard enough for the sound to be heard.

This gesture may look similar to a "want to fight" gesture in the West. Don't worry if you see someone directing this gesture at you. There is no need to move away. No one wants to start a fight with you. In fact, it is quite the opposite. They are agreeing with what you say!

・・・・・・・・・・・・・・・・・・・・・・・・・・・・・

　握りこぶしで、もう片方の手のひらを打つ。

　両太ももをたたくジェスチャーも同じ意味を持つ。このときは、音が聞こえるぐらい、太ももを強くたたく。

　このジェスチャーは、欧米の「けんかをしよう」というジェスチャーに似ている。あなたがだれかからこのジェスチャーをされても、驚かないようにしたい。逃げる必要はない。だれもあなたとけんかをしたいわけではないからだ。実際には、正反対である。あなたの言っていることに賛成しているのだ。

18 | Peek
のぞく
Nozoku

Place your slightly rounded hand against your forehead.

When you see someone making the above gesture, he usually means "looking far away." Some people may stretch the bottom of the nose while making the "looking far away" gesture.

When children make a peek gesture, they may make tubes of their fingers and pretend to be looking through binoculars.

・・・・・・・・・・・・・・・・・・・・・・・・・・・・・・・

　すこし丸めた手を、額の前に置く。

　人がこのジェスチャーをしているときは、ふつう「遠くを見る」という意味になる。この「遠くを見る」ジェスチャーをしながら、鼻の下を伸ばす人もいる。

　子どもが「のぞく」ジェスチャーをするときは、指を筒状にして、双眼鏡で見るまねをすることもある。

19 | Looks delicious!
おいしそう！
Oishi so!

Slide the back of one hand along the curve of the chin, or pretend to wipe off some drool.

This is a *manga*-like expression and rarely seen on formal occasions. However, when some beautiful lady is cooking a special dinner for you, she may be happy to see you make this gesture.

....

　あごの曲線にそって片手の甲をすべらせたり、よだれをぬぐうふりをしたりする。

　マンガチックなジェスチャーで、改まった場でみることはめったにない。しかし、人があなたのために特別なディナーを準備してくれているときは、このジェスチャーをすると、作っている人はうれしくなるだろう。

20 | Got it made!
左うちわ
Hidari uchiwa

Fanning (an *uchiwa* is a fan) yourself slowly with your left (*hidari*) hand.

This gesture indicates a comfortable life. It can also mean that you are congratulating yourself, or that you are easygoing and relaxed. Other meanings include "I'm rich," "I don't have to work," and "I'm making a lot of money."

....

　左手でゆっくりあおぐ動作をする。

　このジェスチャーは、快適な暮らしを表す。また、喜びや、気楽にリラックスしていることを表す。ほかに、「わたしは金持ちだ」「働かなくてよい」「大金を得られそう」といった意味にもなる。

21 | Just hopping mad
おかんむり
Okanmuri

Point both index fingers above your head like horns, as in the horns of an ogre.

In Japan, this gesture is called *okanmuri*. When a married man says "*okanmuri*" while making this gesture, there is a good chance that he means his wife is angry.

This gesture is only used when referring to someone else.

・・・・・・・・・・・・・・・・・・・・・・・・・・・・・・

　両手の人さしゆびを角のように頭上に置く。鬼の角のように見える。

　日本では、このジェスチャーは「おかんむり」と呼ばれている。既婚男性が「おかんむり」と言ってこのジェスチャーをするときは、おそらく奥さんが怒っているのだろう。

　このジェスチャーは、他人のことをいう時にのみ用いる。

22 | Ghost
おばけ
Obake

General Gestures 53

Hang both hands downwards with the backs facing forwards.

The gesture resembles something that has had all the life sucked out of it. Do you think the choreographer of "Thriller" got its dance idea from this? Japanese ghosts, however, wouldn't dance or move like "Thriller" dancers.

....

　手の甲を前にして、両手をだらんと下げる。

　このジェスチャーは、生気をすっかり抜かれてしまった存在に似ている。マイケル・ジャクソンの「スリラー」の振付師は、このポーズからインスピレーションを得たのだろうか。しかし、日本のお化けは、「スリラー」のダンサーのような踊りはしないだろう。

23 | Pointing a finger
ゆびを指す
Yubi wo sasu

A Japanese will point his finger at you to indicate "you." Since words such as you, I, and names are often omitted when speaking Japanese, the subject is sometimes made clear by pointing at it. It is not a popular practice in the West, but is by no means considered rude in Japan.

....

　日本人は、「あなた」を指すときに、指をあなたに向ける。「あなた」「私」、あるいは人名は、日本語で話すときには省かれることが多く、指をさすことで主語をはっきりさせる場合がある。欧米ではあまり見られない慣わしだが、日本では失礼とは思われていない。

24 | No, that's not the case.

そんなことないです。
Sonna koto nai desu.

Shake one or both hands with the palm facing the other person.

This gesture is mostly used when denying a compliment.

It means "Oh, not me" or "I don't deserve such a compliment" and to express modesty or a lack of self-confidence.

....

　片手か両手で、手のひらを相手に向けて振る。

　このジェスチャーは、褒め言葉を否定するときに使うことが多い。

　「いや、私なんか」、あるいは、「私にはもったいないお褒めの言葉です」といった意味で、謙遜や、自信のなさを表す。

25 | This way please. Please sit here.

こちらへどうぞ。 こちらにお座りください。
Kochira e dozo. *Kochira ni osuwari kudasai.*

Show the palm of your hand to the other person and motion with it to the place you wish to indicate.

This is the most polite way to indicate where a person should go or sit. The fingers are together and the tip of the middle finger is directed at the person's feet and the place where he should walk or take a seat. The direction of one's eyes is an important part of this gesture. The person showing the way will look downward in the direction being indicated. This gesture is often seen at temples, shrines, traditional Japanese style hotels, or at Japanese restaurants.

....

　手のひらを相手に見せて、相手を導きたい場所の方へと手ぶりで示す。

　人に行くべき場所や座る場所を示すときの、いちばん礼儀正しい方法である。指をくっつけて、中ゆびの先を、相手の足と、通路や座る場所へと向ける。道を示す場合は、手で示した方向に視線を向ける。このジェスチャーは、寺や神社、伝統的な日本旅館、和食の店などで目にすることが多い。

26 | Line of vision
視線
Shisen

In Western culture, one looks directly into the eyes of the other person. This is not the custom in Japan. On the contrary, it is thought impolite to look directly at a person for an extended period of time.

Most people, in fact, would feel uncomfortable being looked at for a long time unless they were in an intimate relationship with that person.

Also, it would probably work against one to keep looking at a woman in hopes of picking her up at a cafe or such.

This is also used in Japan to mean "to look" as when one looks at something so intently that one forgets the time or when one just keeps looking at something for an extended period of time, as in "to look at it enough to bore a hole in it." This expression gives an indication of how strongly Japanese feel about visibility.

Also, when a Japanese person is focused on a conversation, there are times when the eyes are closed in deep thought, not a custom seen in other countries. It does not mean the person has fallen asleep.

・・・・・・・・・・・・・・・・・・・・・・・・・・・・・・・

　欧米の文化では、他人の目をまっすぐ見つめる。この習慣は日本にはない。それどころか、長い間一人の人をまっすぐ見つめることは、礼儀に反すると考えられている。

　ほとんどの人は、相手と親密な関係にある場合を除いて、長い間見つめられると居心地が悪く感じるだろう。

　また、お茶に誘おうと思って女性をずっと見つめていても、おそらくうまくいかない。

　日本では、長い間じっと見つめていて時間を忘れるぐらいだった、あるいは、長く何かを見つめ続けるときに「穴が開くほど見つめる」といった言い方をすることもある。この表現から、日本人が見られることについてどう感じているかがわかる。

　さらに、日本人が会話に集中すると、目を閉じて考えに沈むことがある。これは他の国では見られない慣わしだが、寝ているわけではない。

Slang Gestures
スラング・ジェスチャー

Discriminatory gestures
Yes, these do exist in Japan as well.
Though it's not advisable to use them too often they are good for a laugh!

差別的なジェスチャー
差別的なジェスチャーは、日本にも存在する。
多用はすすめないが、笑いを取るにはいい。

Explanation of slang star
★ ★ ★ ★ ★

For the chapter on Slang Gestures, we have used stars to indicate the strength of the meaning conveyed. The more stars, the more angry a person may become if you direct the gesture at him.

スラング評価の説明

スラング・ジェスチャーの章では、伝わる意味の強さを示すために星評価を用いた。星が多くなるほど、ジェスチャーをされた人は怒る。

27 | Stupid
くるくるパー
Kuru kuru paa

Turn a closed fist twice while point the index finger at your temple.

Just turning the fist means the same thing but following that by opening the hand facing up increases the degree of stupidity being indicated. It will also increase the anger of the person this gesture is directed at. Opening your hand more strongly and slowly adds to the effect and merits a 10 star rating. If you see someone tapping his temple with the tip of his index finger several times, it means, "Have you gone mad?" This gesture does not mean "to think" as it does in the West. It rates a ★★★☆☆.

....

　人さしゆびをこめかみに向けながら、握りこぶしを2回まわす。

　握りこぶしをまわすだけでも同じ意味になるが、まわした後に手を開き、手のひらを見せることで、ばかにする度合いが上がり、ジェスチャーをされた人の怒りも増すだろう。手をさらに強く、ゆっくり開けば、効果も増し、★10個になる。人さしゆびでこめかみを何度かたたくと、「気が違ったのか」という意味になる。欧米のように、「考える」という意味にはならない。このジェスチャーの評価は★★★☆☆。

28 | To be proud of   To be conceited
鼻が高い   てんぐ
Hana ga takai   *Tengu*

★ ★ ★ ☆ ☆

Make a fist, knuckles up, and place it on the tip on one's nose (for added effect, put both fists one after the other).

This expression and the gesture means "to be proud of something" and "to have confidence in oneself." When a person is called a *tengu* it means he or she is conceited. The long-nosed *tengu* is a mythological spirit believed to live in the mountains.

....

　こぶしを握り、持ち上げて、鼻の先にのせる(効果を増すには、両手のこぶしを重ねる)。

　この表現やジェスチャーには、「何かを誇りに思う」、そして「自信がある」という意味がある。人のことを「てんぐ」と言うとき、その人がうぬぼれていることを意味する。鼻の長いてんぐは、山の中に住むと信じられている神話上の存在である。

29 | Ugly
ブス
Busu

Push up the nostrils with the index finger.

This comes from the notion that an upturned nose is an ugly feature. It is mostly used to convey the appearance of a woman.

In Japan, it is thought embarrassing to show wide-open nostrils to others. The pig in Japan is a symbol of ugly and dirty things. Comedians and actors, when wishing to indicate an ugly person or express that they are playing an ugly person, will sometimes tape the tip of their noses to their foreheads and even color their nostrils black. When you want to make fun of a fat person in Japanese you can say "*buta-yaro*" (you fat jerk) or "*buta*" (pig). This expression warrants a rating of five stars.

....

　鼻孔を人さしゆびで持ち上げる。

　上向きの鼻は醜い顔、という考えかたに由来する。女性の見た目についてのメッセージを伝えるために用いることが多い。

　日本では、広がった鼻孔を他人に見せるのは恥ずかしいことと考えられている。ブタは、日本では醜く汚いものの象徴である。お笑い芸人や俳優たちが、醜い人のことを示したり、醜い人を演じていることを表現したりしたいときには、鼻の先から額にテープを張り、ときには鼻孔を黒く塗ることさえある。太っている人をからかいたいときには、「ブタ野郎」や「ブタ」と言う。この表現は、★★★★★評価を保証する。

30 | Buckteeth
出っ歯
Deppa

★ ★ ☆ ☆ ☆

Cup your hand in front of your mouth with the fingers straight and pointed at a downward angle from your face.

There are many Japanese celebrities who are popular because of their buckteeth and so, in Japan, being bucktoothed may not stop you from enjoying a storybook romance. Not so long ago, a sharp, protruding incisor was considered a cute feature for women. Thus, there were pop idols in the '80s with vampire-like fangs.

・・・・・・・・・・・・・・・・・・・・・・・・・・・

口の前で手を丸め、指を伸ばして顔から下に向ける。

日本には、出っ歯で有名なタレントが多いため、日本では、出っ歯であってもおとぎ話のロマンスを問題なく楽しめる。鋭く突きだした切歯(せっし)が女性のかわいらしい顔立ちだと考えられていたのは、それほど昔のことではない。80年代には、吸血鬼のような牙のポップ・アイドルもいた。

31 | Pregnant
妊娠
Ninshin

Make a half circle with both hands or one hand in front of your stomach.

This gesture is not recommended to be performed in front of women since it also means you have gotten a girl pregnant. In Japan, pregnant women are treated very nicely, even better than mothers with small children. When you want to sit in a crowded train or wish to receive great hospitality, we highly recommend putting a ball under your shirt.

....

　両手か片手で、お腹の前に半円を描く。

　女性を孕(はら)ませたという意味にもなるので、このジェスチャーを女性の前でするのはおすすめしない。日本では、妊婦はよい待遇を受ける。小さい子供連れの母親よりもよい扱いだ。混みあった電車で座りたかったり、親切ていねいにしてもらいたかったりしたら、シャツの下にボールを入れておくことを大いにおすすめしたい。

32 | Big talk
ほらばなし
Hora banashi

★ ☆ ☆ ☆ ☆

Open and close your hand in front of your mouth, bending your wrist slightly back when your hand is closed, and pushing your hand forward as you open it.

Even when you are in a strange land and feel unusually confident, don't talk too big, like saying you're a millionaire back home, or make other foolish *o-bora* (a huge *hora banashi*). And if you are a married man, don't make too much *hora* about being single in an attempt to be a hit with the girls!

・・・・・・・・・・・・・・・・・・・・・・・・・・・・

　口の前で手を開閉し、手を閉じるときに手首を少し後ろに曲げ、開くときに手を前に押し出す。

　見知らぬ土地にいていつもより気が大きくなっていても、故郷では億万長者だとか、くだらない大ぼらを吹くのはやめよう。既婚の男性なら、女の子にモテようとして、独身だとほらを吹くのもたいがいにしたい。

33 | I doubt it!
まゆつばもの
Mayu tsuba mono

★ ★ ★ ☆ ☆

Mayu = eyebrow, *tsuba* = saliva, *mono* = thing

This is a gesture where you lick the tip of your middle finger and run it across your eyebrow.

You would do this when you doubt what you are hearing.

A *mayu tsuba mono* is something that may deceive you and about which you want to be cautious.

The gesture has many possible origins, but the most popular is from traditional folk tales, where a fox or a *tanuki* (raccoon dog) often disguises itself as a human in order to deceive them. Its magic, however, is rendered powerless when saliva gets on its eyebrow. The gesture has a long history, and is said to have been used since the *Heian* Period.

....

　これは、中ゆびの先をなめて、まゆの上をすべらせるジェスチャーだ。

　耳にしたことを疑っているときにこの動きをする。

　「まゆつばもの」は、だまされそうなものや、注意しなければならないものを意味する。

　ジェスチャーの起源には諸説あるが、一番ポピュラーなのはキツネやタヌキがよく人に化けて、人間を騙そうとする、という民話にもとづくものだ。しかし、まゆにつばをつけると、幻術は解けてしまう。このジェスチャーには長い歴史があり、平安時代から用いられているということだ。

34 | Those people are in the midst of a fight or argument
喧嘩中
Kenkachu

★ ☆ ☆ ☆ ☆

Make a cross with the index fingers of both hands, then move one finger in front of the other in rapid succession. This imitates fighting with *katana* (Japanese swords).

You will hardly see any Japanese fighting with *katana* in Japan nowadays.

If by any chance, you see people fighting using *katana*, don't just stand there taking photos! Run away at once!

・・・・・・・・・・・・・・・・・・・・・・・・・・・・・

　両手の人さしゆびを交差し、片方の指をもう片方の指の前にすばやく連続して動かす。これは、刀での戦いをまねたものだ。

　今日の日本で、日本人が刀で戦うのを目にすることはまずないだろう。

　もし刀で戦う人を目にしたら、そこで突っ立って写真を撮っていてはいけない。すぐに逃げるようにしよう！

35 | Gay
おかま
Okama

★ ★ ☆ ☆ ☆

This gesture means gay if you remain silent.

If you say something, it means that you are whispering about someone behind his or her back.

Gay TV personalities are becoming very popular in Japan among Japanese women. The type of gay men popular in Japan do not have a particular look, but tend to be people who give critical advice on women's fashion.

・・

　このジェスチャーは、黙っていればゲイを意味する。

　何かを言えば、他人の陰口を言うことを意味する。

　日本では、ゲイのタレントは日本人女性の間で人気が高まっている。日本で人気のあるゲイ男性のタイプは、ルックスに特徴があるわけではないが、女性ファッションの批評やアドバイスをする人が多い。

36 | Japanese mafia
やくざ
Yakuza

Pretend to draw a line with the nail of your index finger from the ear to the chin.

This indicates a scar gotten from fighting or such.

In general, *yakuza* (Japanese mafia) value traditions, are well behaved and respect their elders. Be sure to be on your best behavior when meeting them.

....

　耳からあごに、人さしゆびのつめで線を引くふりをする。

　けんかなどでついた傷を示すジェスチャーである。

　一般的に、やくざはしきたりを重んじ、行儀がよく、年長者を敬う。やくざに会ったら、よい振る舞いをするようにしよう。

37 | To be arrested
逮捕
Taiho

★ ☆ ☆ ☆ ☆

Lightly make fists of both hands and place both wrists together (as if being handcuffed).

When making this sign to someone who already has a criminal record it warrants a ★ ★ ★ ★ ☆ rating.

....
両手を軽くにぎって、
(手錠をかけられたように)手首を合わせる。

犯罪歴のある人にむかってこのジェスチャーをしたら、
★★★★☆を保証する。

38 | Shoplift
万引き
Manbiki

★ ★ ★ ☆ ☆

Crook the upright index finger.

You can move the finger up and down if you like.

Doesn't this gesture remind you of the famous Captain with a Hook?

....

突き立てた人さしゆびを曲げる。

何なら、人さしゆびを上下してもよい。

このジェスチャーは、有名なキャプテン・フックを連想しないだろうか。

39 | You want me to punch you?
なぐってやろうか？
Nagutte yaro ka?

★ ★ ★ ☆ ☆

Blow on the fist or shake the fist at the opponent.

This is often used as a friendly gesture. Don't worry. The person making the gesture will not really start a fight with you.

....

　拳に息をふきかけたり、拳を相手に向けて振ったりする。

　フレンドリーなジェスチャーとして使われることが多いから、心配は無用だ。このジェスチャーをしている人が、本当にあなたとけんかをするわけではない。

40 | Abject apology
土下座
Dogeza

☆ ☆ ☆ ☆ ☆

Kneeling before someone. A gesture of deep apology toward someone you have angered or when you are making a very serious request.

Kneel with the upper body bent over the knees, head bowed to the floor in a gesture of deep respect or gravest apology. It is also a sign of humility and subservience. You must do this when begging forgiveness for an irrevocable mistake. Put your forehead to the ground and keep it there until the other person tells you to lift your head. If you are a hip-hop dancer, the position just might prompt you to lift your legs and start spinning around on your head. However, as this will fail to demonstrate remorse, it will likely earn you five stars!

． ．

　人の前にひざまずく。怒らせた相手への心からの謝罪や、一大事をお願いするときのジェスチャー。

　深い尊敬や最大級の謝罪を表すジェスチャーとして、ひざまずいて上半身を曲げ、頭を床に向けて下げる。また、謙虚や卑屈を示すジェスチャーでもある。取り返しのつかない過ちをしたときに許しを乞うには、土下座をしなければならない。額を床につけて、相手が頭を上げなさいと言うまでその姿勢を保つようにする。ヒップホップダンサーなら、脚を上げて、ヘッドスピンをはじめたくなる態勢かもしれない。しかしそんなことをしたら反省の色を示せず、きっと★★★★★の怒りを買うだろう。

41 | Vavavoom!
ハナヂ、ぶ〜！
Hanaji buuuu!

Cover your nostrils with your index and middle fingers, and very quickly, in a forceful movement, like water spurting out from a faucet, bring your fingers down past your chin. Or push them out in front of you as though something is pouring out.

This is a comical gesture expressing blood gushing out of your nose. You would do this jokingly, for example, when you see someone of the opposite sex who is totally your type, someone who would make you so excited that blood rushes to your head and cause your nose to start bleeding.

It is not so much an offensive gesture for the other person. Too bad there aren't more times that call for it.

★ ☆ ☆ ☆ ☆

　鼻孔を人さしゆびと中ゆびで覆い、それからとても素早く、力強く、水が蛇口から吹き出すように、指をあごの下へと持っていく。あるいは、何かが湧き出るように、目の前に指を押し出す。

　これは、鼻から血が吹き出てくる様子を表すコミカルなジェスチャーである。たとえば、自分のタイプそのものの異性に会い、舞い上がって頭に血が上り、鼻血が出てきそうなときに、ジョークとしてやるといいだろう。

　このジェスチャーは、相手をあまり怒らせない。使うのにふさわしい場面がもっとあればいいのに、と思う。

42 | Butter someone up
ごますり
Goma suri

★ ☆ ☆ ☆ ☆

Rotate one fist on top of the open palm of the other hand.

Derived from the motion of grinding sesame seeds with a mortar and pestle. Used to signify singing the praises of another person, usually in anticipation of something in return.

・・・・・・・・・・・・・・・・・・・・・・・・・・・・・

　握りこぶしを、もう片方の手のひらの上で回転させる。

　すり鉢とすりこぎでゴマの種をすりつぶす動きに由来する。たいていは見返りを求めて、人を褒めそやす意味で使われる。

43 | Boyfriend
彼氏
Kareshi

★ ☆ ☆ ☆ ☆

Point your thumb upright.

Kareshi means a steady boyfriend.

This gesture is categorized as slang, but would not be considered impolite if used in front of others.

Not recommended to be used by women.

. . . .

親ゆびを立てる。

「彼氏」は、付き合っている男友達を意味する。

このジェスチャーはスラングに分類されているが、他人のいる前で使っても失礼とは思われない。

女性がするのはお勧めしない。

44 | Girlfriend
彼女
Kanojo

★ ☆ ☆ ☆ ☆

Point your pinkie upright.

Kanojo means a steady girlfriend.

This gesture is categorized as slang, but would not be considered impolite if used in front of others.

Not recommended to be used by women.

....

小ゆびを立てる。

「彼女」は、付き合っている女友達を意味する。

このジェスチャーはスラングに分類されているが、他人のいる前で使っても失礼とは思われない。

女性がするのはお勧めしない。

45 | Sex

セックス
Sekkusu

In America, this gesture is the letter "T" in sign language. In the olden days in Japan, it meant "sex." This gesture already existed in the *Edo* Period and was quite popular. It was also said to have been used before the *Edo* Period. However, now in the time of *Heisei*, this gesture is considered vulgar. It is hardly seen anymore although many Japanese do know and understand the meaning. In some regions, the thumb sticking out between the index and middle finger symbolized a penis. Also, some people use the thumb sticking out between the middle and ring finger to mean "breast."

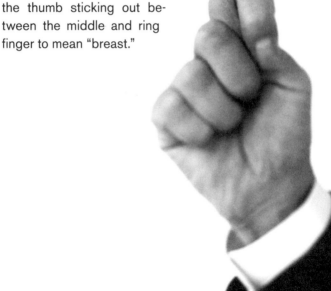

★ ★ ★ ★ ★

In any case, these gestures are all rather crude and considered vulgar in most parts of Asia. However, in Brazil a country right behind Japan (see the globe if you don't believe it), this gesture means "good luck and happiness." So, in Brazil, you can find key holders and many other items made in this shape.

・・・・・・・・・・・・・・・・・・・・・・・・・・・・

　アメリカでは、このジェスチャーは手話の「T」の字を意味する。昔の日本では、「セックス」を意味していた。江戸時代にはすでに存在し、大いに用いられていた。江戸時代より前に使われていたとも言われている。平成の現在では、卑猥とされ、ほとんど目にすることはなくなっているが、多くの日本人はその意味を知っている。一部の地域では、人さしゆびと中ゆびの間から突き出す親ゆびがペニスを意味する。また、中ゆびと薬ゆびの間から親ゆびを突き出して「胸」を意味する人もいる。

　とにかく、アジアの大部分の地域では、こういったジェスチャーはみな、下品で野卑なものと考えられている。しかし、日本の正反対にあるブラジル（嘘だと思ったら地球儀を見てみよう）では、このジェスチャーは「幸運と幸せ」を表す。だから、ブラジルでは、キーホルダーなど多くのものがこの形をしている。

46 | How about a drink?
一杯どう？
Ippai do?

☆ ☆ ☆ ☆ ☆

Extend your thumb and index finger (like the letter "c") and hold them horizontally, as if you were holding an *ochoko*, a small cup used to drink *sake*.

This gesture is categorized as slang, but is not considered impolite. It is mainly used by men. Men would make this gesture when asking a co-worker for a drink after work. It could also be used when asking women.

・・・・・・・・・・・・・・・・・・・・・・・・・・・・・

　親ゆびと人さしゆびを(「c」の文字のように)伸ばして、お酒を飲むおちょこを持っているかのように水平に保つ。

　このジェスチャーはスラングに分類されているが、他人のいる前で使っても失礼とは思われない。主に男性によって用いられる。仕事の後で同僚を飲みに誘うときに、男性はこのジェスチャーをする。女性を誘うときにも用いられることがある。

47 | Was fired.
クビになりました。
Kubi ni nari mashita.

★ ★ ★ ☆ ☆

Extend the back of your hand horizontally and slide it in front of the neck as if you were cutting off your head.

This gesture is used when talking about someone that has been fired. When you make this gesture to a person who has, in fact, been fired, it warrants a ★ ★ ★ ★ ★ rating.

....

手の甲を水平に伸ばし、頭が切り落とされるように、首の前で横にすべらせる。

このジェスチャーは、仕事をクビになった人について話すときに用いられる。実際にクビになった人にこのジェスチャーをしたら、★★★★★効果となることを保証する。

48 | Money　　Condom
お金　　コンドーム
Okane　　*Kondomu*

Money

Condom

Slang Gestures 107

★ ★ ☆ ☆ ☆

Make a circle with your thumb and index finger (the Western "OK") and hold it flat, horizontally.

If this gesture is made in a drugstore it means a condom. The condom can be expressed with the OK sign, in other words, the hand does not have to be held horizontally.

・・・・・・・・・・・・・・・・・・・・・・・・・・・・

　親ゆびと人さしゆびで丸印を作り（欧米では「OKの意味」）、手を平らに、水平にする。これは「お金」の意味となる。

　このジェスチャーを薬局ですれば、コンドームの意味になる。コンドームは、OKのサインで表せる。つまり、手を水平に保つ必要はない。

49 | Bribe
ワイロ
Wairo

★ ★ ★ ☆ ☆

Imitating hiding money inside the collar of the *kimono*. Nowadays, since the majority of Japanese no longer wear *kimono*, this gesture is seen as pretending to hide money inside one's inner suit pocket. Bribery still exists in Japan even though we no longer wear *kimono*.

If you see someone making this gesture and repeatedly opening and closing one side of the jacket, it means he's making tons. He will usually say "*gappo gappo*" while doing this. *Gappo gappo* expresses the millions of yen sliding into his sleeve.

....

　着物の襟もとに金を隠すまねをする。今日では、日本人の多くは着物を着ていないため、このジェスチャーは、スーツの内ポケットにお金を隠すふりだと考えられている。日本人はもう着物を着ないが、ワイロは依然として日本に存在している。

　人がこのジェスチャーをして、上着の片側を何度も開け閉めするのは、大金を稼いでいるという意味だ。その人は、このジェスチャーをしながら「がっぽがっぽ」と言うのが普通である。「がっぽがっぽ」というのは、何百万円もの大金が袂に転がり込んでくる様子を表現している。

Children's Gestures
子どものジェスチャー

Expressions used in manga (comics) or manga-like expressions.

These are cute gestures used by children and are derived from TV or comics.

マンガで使われる表現やマンガチックな表現。

子どもたちが使うキュートなジェスチャーで、テレビやマンガ由来のものである。

50 | Pedestrian crossing
横断歩道
Odan hodo

Crossing the crosswalk with one arm up-stretched.

In order to prevent accidents, schools require children to do this when crossing the street so that they are easily visible to drivers. Some districts even leave yellow flags on either side of crosswalks so children can carry them as they cross the street.

A raised arm does not mean that a pedestrian wants a car to stop in the middle of the road or that he wants to say something to the driver. And even though children may be waving flags, it doesn't mean they're surrendering.

....

　片腕をまっすぐ上に伸ばして横断歩道を渡る。

　ドライバーがよく見えるようにして事故を防ぐために、子どもたちが横断歩道を渡るときにこうするよう学校は義務づけている。地区によっては、横断歩道の両側に黄色の旗を置いて、道を横切るときに旗を持っていけるようにしているところもある。

　腕を上げていても、歩行者が道の真中で車を止めたがっていたり、ドライバーに何かを言いたかったりしているわけではない。子どもたちが旗を振っていても、降伏するという意味ではない。

51 | Counting
かぞえかた
Kazoe kata

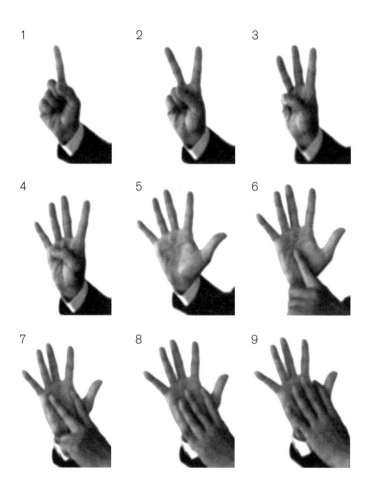

Children's Gestures 115

Use the fingers to express the numbers one to ten by holding up the corresponding number of fingers.

....

指を使い、数の分だけ指を上げることで、
1から10までの数を表す。

10

52 | Finger Family
ゆび家族
Yubi kazoku

Thumb – 親ゆび *Oya yubi*

Oya means parent; *yubi* means finger, that is why a thumb is called *oya yubi*.

親は「両親」、ゆびは「指」の意味。

Pointing finger – 人さしゆび *Hito sashi yubi*

Hito means person; *sashi* means to point; *yubi* means finger, therefore the index finger is called *hito sashi yubi*.

人は「人間」、さしは「指さす」、ゆびは「指」の意味。

Middle finger – 中ゆび *Naka yubi*

Naka means center or middle; *yubi* means finger, therefore the middle finger is called *naka yubi*.

中は「中心、真ん中」、ゆびは「指」の意味。

Ring finger – 薬ゆび *Kusuri yubi*

Kusuri means medicine; *yubi* means finger. The word *kusuri yubi* comes from the custom in the olden days of using the ring finger to mix medicine. The ring finger was also called *beni sashi yubi* (*beni sashi* means to apply lipstick) because it was also used to apply lipstick.

薬は「薬品」、ゆびは「指」の意味。
薬ゆびの由来は、昔このゆびで薬を調合していたことに由来する。薬ゆびは「紅差しゆび」（紅差しは、口紅を塗るという意味）とも言うが、これは、薬ゆびが口紅を塗るためにも使われていたから。

Small finger – 小ゆび *Ko yubi*

The word for small is *ko*; *yubi* means finger, therefore the small finger is called *ko yubi*.

小は「小さい、かわいい」の意味。ゆびは「指」の意味。

Children express family members with their fingers.
The thumb is the father finger. The index finger is the mother.
The middle finger is the brother. The ring finger is the sister.
The small finger is the baby.

子どもたちは、指で家族を表現する。
親ゆびは父親の指。人さしゆびは母親。
中ゆびが兄弟。薬ゆびが姉妹。
そして小ゆびが赤ん坊である。

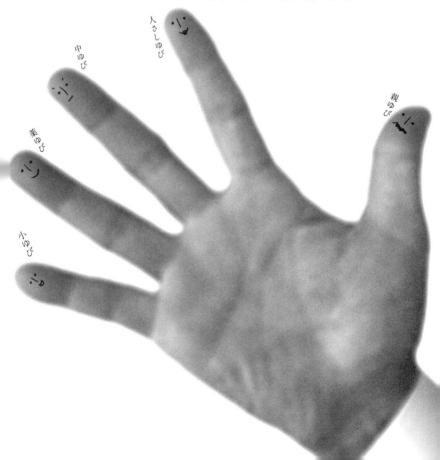

53 | Making a vow using your fingers
ゆびきり
Yubi kiri

This gesture is made while singing a song. Children sing while intertwining each other's pinkies of one hand.

The words to the song "*Yubi kiri genman*," mean "if you lie, I will make you swallow 1,000 needles" are pretty scary. In the Japanese mafia, breaking a promise or making some other transgression usually requires that the first digit of a finger, usually the pinkie, be cut off.

・・・・・・・・・・・・・・・・・・・・・・・・・・・・・

　このジェスチャーは、歌いながら行う。子どもは、片方の小ゆびをお互いに絡み合わせながら歌う。

　「指きりげんまん」の歌詞は、「嘘をついたら、針を1000本飲ませるぞ」という意味で、なかなか恐ろしい。日本のやくざは、約束を破るなどの罪を犯すと、指（ふつうは小ゆび）の第一関節を切断しなければならないのが普通である。

54 | Please!   Sorry.
お願い！ ごめん。
Onegai! *Gomen.*

Place both palms together.

This is a gesture used when saying "sorry," or when accepting something while feeling apologetic for having inconvenienced the other person. Although this is a polite gesture, it is usually considered somewhat effeminate. In Japan, the word "*gomen*" is not only an expression of apology but expresses politeness. For instance, in asking a favor, many Japanese would start by saying, "*Gomen*..." This could be translated as "I need a favor, but...," "Could you help me?"

When you see Japanese making this gesture, remember, it doesn't mean they're losers, just that they're simply very polite!

....

　両手のひらを合わせる。

　相手に迷惑をかけて申し訳ないという気持ちで、「ごめんなさい」というときや、何かを受け入れるときに使うジェスチャーである。礼儀ただしいジェスチャーだが、普通は女々しいと思われてしまう。日本では、「ごめん」という言葉は、謝罪だけでなく、敬意も表す。例えば、お願いをするとき、多くの日本人は「ごめん…」という言葉からはじめる。これは、「お願いがあるのですが…」「助けてもらえませんか」という意味に解される。

　日本人がこのジェスチャーをしているときは、負け犬なのではなく、単に敬意を払っているだけであることを忘れないようにしよう。

55 | Grab this finger!
このゆびとーまれ！
Kono yubi tomare!

Children's Gestures

When a child wants to start a game with his friends, he will point his index finger up and yell, "*Kono yubi tomare*," or "grab this finger."

Those who want to join in will gather around like bees swarming around a flower, and start grabbing at the finger. If a child grabs your finger when you point it upward to signify the Western "wait!" you will now know that it's because he thinks you are starting a game.

Personally, I would have liked to see someone do this to John Travolta in "Saturday Night Fever" when he made that famous pose. Actually, though, this gesture is usually only made with the finger raised to chest level.

....

子どもが友達と遊びをはじめたいときに、人さしゆびを立てて、「このゆびとーまれ」と叫ぶ。

遊びに加わりたい子どもたちは、花の蜜に群がるハチのように集まって、指を掴み始める。欧米では指を上に向けると「待ちなさい」という意味になるが、日本人の子どもがその指をつかんだら、あなたが遊びを始めたいと思ったからだというのが、今ならわかるだろう。

個人的には、「サタデー・ナイト・フィーバー」でジョン・トラボルタがあの有名なポーズをしたときに、誰かが指をつかむのを見たかったなと思う。しかし実際には、このジェスチャーでは普通、指を胸の高さまでしか上げない。

56 | Aren't I cute?
かわいい？
Kawaii?

Smiling and looking up slightly, touch both index fingers lightly to your cheeks while tilting the head a bit to the side. The gesture can be made with one hand as well.

This is an old expression and was often used by children before the "peace" sign (the "V" sign made with the middle and index finger) became popular.

・・・・・・・・・・・・・・・・・・・・・・・・・・・・・

　ほほえみ、軽く上目づかいで、両手の人さしゆびを軽くほほにつけて、頭を片方に軽く傾ける。このジェスチャーは、片手でも行うことができる。

　これは古くからのジェスチャーで、「ピース」のサイン（中ゆびと人さしゆびで「V」字サインを作る）が流行るまでは、子どもがよくやっていた。

57 | You are so silly!

おしりぺんぺん！
Oshiri pen pen!

Oshiri pen pen is the sound of spanking the bottom lightly.

Showing the bottom to another person and patting it is used to ridicule.

・・・・・・・・・・・・・・・・・・・・・・・・・・・・・・・

おしりぺんぺんは、おしりを軽くたたくときの音である。

人におしりを見せて、たたくジェスチャーは、
人をからかうときに用いる。

58 | Na-nana-na-na.
あっかんべー。
Akkanbeee.

Sticking out the tongue
舌を出す
Shita wo dasu

Pull down the lower lid of one eye with the index finger while you say "*akkan*" and stick out the tongue as you say "*beee.*"

This means "Ugh, I've had it." or "I don't like you." This gesture is equivalent to the taunting "Na-nana-na-na" in the West.

A Japanese girl may stick out her tongue jokingly when she makes a small blunder or slip-up. The gesture can be roughly translated as the English expression "Uh-oh!"

目の下まぶたを人さしゆびで引っ張って「あっかん」と言い、それから舌を突き出して「ベー」と言う。

「ああ、もううんざり」や、「お前のこときらい」といった意味になる。このジェスチャーは、アメリカの「ナーナナ ナーナー」というからかい言葉と同じ意味である。

日本の女の子は、ちょっとドジを踏んだり間違えたりしたら、ふざけて舌を出すことがある。このジェスチャーは、英語の「オッォー」という表現におおむね相当する。

59 | Rock-paper-scissors!
じゃんけん
Jan ken

Commonly done when randomly selecting a person for some purpose, such as deciding the order of players in a game.

Chanting "*jan, ken, pon,*" on "*pon*" the players make one of three shapes with their fists:

Choki = scissors
Pa = paper
Gu = rock

Scissors can cut paper, so scissors win. But scissors can't cut rock, so it loses to rock. And since paper covers a rock, paper wins.

....

　遊びのプレイヤーの順番を決めるときなど、ある目的で一人をランダムに選ぶときによく行われる。

　「じゃんけんぽん」と歌いながら、「ぽん」でプレイヤーは拳の形を次の3つのうちの1つにする。

　チョキ＝はさみ
　パー＝紙
　グー＝岩

　はさみは紙を切ることができるので、はさみが勝つ。しかし、はさみは岩を切ることができないので、岩には負ける。紙は岩をおおうので、紙が勝つ。

60 | They're deeply in love!
あちち！
Achichi!

Bend the index fingers of both hands and bring them together several times.

This gesture is often used when a couple is seen being cuddly in public. It's fairly outdated but is still understood.

Achichi can also be roughly translated as "they're hot" in English. This gesture is often used by children to tease young couples. It would not be used toward a husband and wife or toward elderly couples.

　両手の人さしゆびを折り曲げて、何度かくっつける。

　このジェスチャーは、カップルが人前でいちゃいちゃしているときによく使う。だいぶ古くなったが、まだ通じる。

　「あちち」は、「二人」が「熱い」関係にあるという意味に近い。このジェスチャーは、子どもが若いカップルをからかうときによく使われる。既婚の夫婦や、中高年のカップルには使われない。

61 | Flower
花
Hana

Children's Gestures 135

Spread your fingers wide and place the base of your palms together in a flower-like ring.

In elementary school, children are often asked to make the flower gesture when receiving a special gift from the teacher and the gesture is often seen when children sing and dance to songs. When you have a chance to see this gesture, we are certain it will make you smile.

....

　指を大きく広げ、手のひらの付け根を合わせて花のような輪の形にする。

　小学校では、先生から特別なプレゼントをもらうときに、この花のジェスチャーをするように言われることが多い。また、子どもたちが歌ったり、歌に合わせて踊ったりするときに、このジェスチャーをよく見る。このジェスチャーを見る機会があったら、きっとほほが緩むだろうと思う。

62 | Your underwear is showing
ぱんつーまるみえ
Pan tsuu maru mie

「*Pan*」

「*Tsuu*」

「*Maru*」

「*Mie*」

Clap both hands saying "*pan*," raise your index and middle finger in a "V" sign saying "*tsu*" (meaning "two" in English), make a circle with your fingers saying "*maru*" (which means "circle"), bring both palms to the side of your face as if to peep and say "*mie*" (meaning "to see"). This gesture is mainly used to make fun of someone but it can also be used to warn an unsuspecting person that his underwear is showing without announcing it publicly.

・・・・・・・・・・・・・・・・・・・・・・・・・・・・・

　「ぱん」と言いながら両手をたたき、人さしゆびと中ゆびを持ち上げて「V」字のサインを作って「つー」(「つー」は英語の「2」を意味する)と言い、指で輪を作って「まる」と言い、最後に片手か両手の手のひらを顔の横に持っていって、覗き見するように「みえ」と言う。このジェスチャーは、人をからかうために使われるのが普通だが、「見せる」と言ってもないのに下着を見せてしまっている、無防備な人に注意するために使われることもある。

63 | Stars shining brightly
お星さまキラキラ
Ohoshisama kira kira

Open your fingers and twist your hands at the wrists above your head to represent stars sparkling brightly.

Try doing the hand motion while singing "Twinkle Twinkle Little Star." You will be amazed how charming you look!

....

　頭のところか頭上で、指を開き、手首のところで手を回転して、まばゆく輝く星を表す。

　「きらきら星」を歌いながら、手を動かすようにする。自分がチャーミングに見えて、きっとびっくりするだろう。

64 | Peace
ピース
Piisu

This does not mean "peace" in the literal sense, but is used more for when striking a pose for a photograph. This may be considered the equivalent of "hang loose" in the U.S.

This gesture is a common pose for photos.

「平和」という文字通りの意味ではなく、写真のポーズを決めるときに使われることが多い。親ゆびと小ゆびでつくるアメリカの「ハング・ルース」(気楽に行こう)というサインと同じようなものとも考えられる。

このジェスチャーは、写真でよく使われるポーズである。

65 | That's that!
えんがちょ！
Engacho!

Make a circle with both index fingers and thumbs and have someone else make a cutting action where your fingers connect.

This is a superstitious gesture that means cutting oneself off from something dirty or unwelcome. Depending on age and region there is said to be two or three different ways of making this gesture. You can see this gesture in the film, "*Spirited Away*" by *Hayao Miyazaki*.

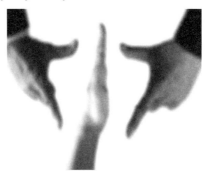

....

　両手の人さしゆびと親ゆびで輪をつくり、他の人に、指がつながっている場所を切るアクションをさせる。

　これは、汚らわしいものや好ましくないものから自分自身を切り離す、という意味の、迷信にまつわるジェスチャーである。年齢や地域によって、このジェスチャーのやり方には2、3のバリエーションがある。宮崎駿の「千と千尋の神隠し」でこのジェスチャーを見ることができる。

66 | Barrier!
バリアー！
Bariaaah!

Make a Peace sign (V sign) with both hands and intertwine the middle finger with the index finger.

This represents a barrier you are raising against dirty things or people you don't want to be contaminated by. It means, "You can't touch me." There are variations of this gesture depending on age and area. Some say this is *engacho*. However, considering where the gesture comes from, we feel the gesture pictured above is the closest to the original. It may have changed according to how children performed it.

The motion of drawing a triangle using both hands in front of you is also a gesture that expresses a barrier!

・・・

　ピースサイン（Vサイン）を片手でして、中ゆびと人さしゆびを絡み合わせる。

　これは、汚らわしいものや、悪い影響を受けたくないと思っている人を遠ざけるバリアーを表し、「私に触ることはできない」という意味になる。このジェスチャーは、年齢や地域によってバリエーションが有る。「えんがちょ」という人もいる。しかし、ジェスチャーの由来を考えると、この写真の形のジェスチャーが一番オリジナルに近いと考えている。子どもたちが実際にやっていく中で変化していったのかもしれない。

　体の前で両手を使って三角形を描く動きも、バリアを表すジェスチャーである！

67 | Passing by a funeral car
霊柩車が通る
Reikyusha ga toru

Hide both thumbs until a funeral car is out of sight.

Because of the saying that one won't be able to see the face of one's parents on their deathbeds, people cover their thumbs, which in Japanese are called *oya* (parent) *yubi* (finger).

This gesture is not used at funerals. It is a superstitious gesture made so one will be able to see the faces of their parents on their deathbeds or wishing that one's parents will not be called by God too soon.

Refer to **52** I Finger Family on p.116

....

霊柩車が見えなくなるまで、両方の親ゆびを隠す。

死に際の親の顔を見ることができなくなるという言い伝えがあるため、日本人は親ゆび(親の指)を隠す。

このジェスチャーは、葬式では用いられない。これは、死に際に親の顔を見ることができるように、あるいは、神の下にあまりに早く召されることがないようにという願いから行われる、縁起かつぎのジェスチャーである。

68 | I'm angry
膨れっ面
Fukurettsura

As a way to communicate their anger, children puff up their cheeks and glower.

The gesture expresses frustration and anger.

This gesture is similar to the facial expression for "fat" in the West. If you see a child making this gesture at you, he in no way means you're fat!

Japanese children will also puff up their cheeks when you say something they don't like, don't want to hear or when they want to complain about something.

Adults use the expression *buu buu iu* (always complaining) when they see children with puffed-up cheeks.

....

　怒りを示すために、子どもはほほをふくらませて赤らめる。

　このジェスチャーは、いらだちや怒りを表す。

　これは、欧米で「太っている」ことを表す表情と似ている。子どもがこのジェスチャーをしてきても、あなたが太っているといいたいわけではない。

　日本の子どもは、あなたが嫌なこと、聞きたくないことを言ったり、何かに不満があったりするときにもほほをふくらませる。

　大人は、子どもがほほをふくらませていると、「ブーブー言う」（いつも文句ばかり言う）という表現を使う。

69 | Hooray!
万歳！
Banzai!

Throwing both arms up while shouting "*banzai*." Expresses good fortune or happiness.

If the arms are not fully extended but are bent at the elbows, it means surrendering.

After a game, the winning team often does three loud *banzais*, which is collectively called "*banzai sansho*." It is similar to "hip hip hooray" in English. *Do age* (throwing a person into the air) is also a common practice after a game made up of men only. Players form a circle, throw one of them in the air, catch him as he comes down, then repeat the throw and catch three or four times. In most cases, *do age* is an act of appreciation to the person being thrown, who is usually the manager or leader of the team or group. If you see this, don't think the people doing this are male cheerleaders!

・・・・・・・・・・・・・・・・・・・・・・・・・・・・・

　両手を放り上げながら、「万歳」と言う。幸運や喜びを表現する。

　腕が完全に伸びきらずに、肘のところで曲げれば、降伏の意味になる。

　ゲームのあと、勝ったチームはよく「万歳」を大声で三回行う。これをまとめて万歳三唱と言う。英語の「ヒップ、ヒップ、フレー！」に似ている。胴上げ（人を空中に放り上げること）も、男だけが参加する試合が終わった後によく見られる。プレイヤーは円陣を組み、仲間の一人を空中に放り投げて、降りてきたら受け止める。この放り投げと受け止めを３、４回繰り返す。たいていの場合、「胴上げ」は放り投げられた人を称える行為であり、チームやグループの監督や指導者が対象になる。胴上げを見ても、男のチアリーダーたちだとは思わないように。

70 | *Gatchohhhhn!*
がちょーーん！
Gatchooooon!

Bring your hand forward as if throwing a ball and keep your hand open while pulling it back and forth while saying "*Gatchohhhhn!*"

A well-known Japanese comedian made this gesture popular in a TV show. Mainly used when something is anticlimactic or the outcome is not as was anticipated.

....

ボールを投げるように手を前に投げ出して、手を開いたまま腕を前後させ、「がちょーん！」と言う。

日本の有名お笑い芸人がテレビ番組でこのジェスチャーをやって有名にした。期待はずれだったり、予想通りの結果が得られなかったりしたときに使われるのが普通である。

Something special for you

Golf
ゴルフ

This is not a gesture but it is often seen in Japan.

One of the most popular sports for Japanese businessmen is golf.

これはジェスチャーではないが、日本でよく見られる。

日本のビジネスマンに一番人気のスポーツのひとつがゴルフである。

Children's Gestures 155

You will often see people standing on the station platform practicing their golf swing with their umbrellas. If you are a golfer yourself, swinging an umbrella is not taboo by any means. However, doing so in a place where space is limited is dangerous, and therefore earns the five stars. Exclusively for men. One never sees women doing this.

　駅のプラットフォームで、傘をスイングしてゴルフの練習をする人をよく見かける。あなた自身がゴルフをするなら、傘をスイングしてもまったく問題ない。しかし、狭い空間ですると危険なので、★★★★★になる。これは男だけの行動である。女性がやっているのを見た人はいない。

Index

General Gestures

01	Bowing	—	*Ojigi* 8
02	Yes. / No.	—	*Hai. / Iie.* 10
03	Thank you. / It was delicious!	—	*Itadakimasu. / Gochisosama.* 12
04	Me	—	*Watashi* 14
05	Come over here! / Go away!	—	*Kocchi ni oide! / Acchi ike!* 16
06	Calm down.	—	*Ochi tsui te* 18
07	I'm going to pass in front of you.	—	*Mae wo tori masu.* 20
08	I don't know. / That's wrong.	—	*Shiranai. / Chigau.* 22
09	Thank you.	—	*Katajikenai.* 24
10	Do you want to go eat?	—	*Shokuji* 26
11	Wait a moment.	—	*Chotto matte.* 28
12	Formal / Indian-style	—	*Seiza / Agura* 30
13	Tapping the shoulder	—	*Kata wo tataku* 34
14	Hot!	—	*Atsui!* 36
15	To laugh	—	*Warau* 38
16	Let's put that subject aside.	—	*Sono hanashi wa oitoi te.* 40
17	I agree!	—	*Nattoku!* 42
18	Peek	—	*Nozoku* 44
19	Looks delicious!	—	*Oishi so!* 46
20	Got it made!	—	*Hidari uchiwa* 48
21	Just hopping mad	—	*Okanmuri* 50
22	Ghost	—	*Obake* 52
23	Pointing a finger	—	*Yubi wo sasu* 54
24	No, that's not the case.	—	*Sonna koto nai desu.* 56
25	This way please. Please sit here.	—	*Kochira e dozo.* *Kochira ni osuwari kudasai.* 58
26	Line of vision	—	*Shisen* 60

Slang Gestures

27	Stupid	—	*Kuru kuru paa* 64
28	To be proud of To be conceited	—	*Hana ga takai* *Tengu* 66
29	Ugly	—	*Busu* 68
30	Buckteeth	—	*Deppa* 70
31	Pregnant	—	*Ninshin* 72
32	Big talk	—	*Hora banashi* 74
33	I doubt it!	—	*Mayu tsuba mono* 76
34	Those people are in the midst of a fight or argument	—	*Kenkachu* 78
35	Gay	—	*Okama* 80
36	Japanese mafia	—	*Yakuza* 82
37	To be arrested	—	*Taiho* 84
38	Shoplift	—	*Manbiki* 86
39	You want me to punch you?	—	*Nagutte yaro ka?* 88
40	Abject apology	—	*Dogeza* 90
41	Vavavoom!	—	*Hanaji buuuu!* 92
42	Butter someone up	—	*Goma suri* 94
43	Boyfriend	—	*Kareshi* 96
44	Girlfriend	—	*Kanojo* 98
45	Sex	—	*Sekkusu* 100
46	How about a drink?	—	*Ippai do?* 102
47	Was fired.	—	*Kubi ni nari mashita.* 104
48	Money / Condom	—	*Okane / Kondomu* 106
49	Bribe	—	*Wairo* 108

Children's Gestures

50	Pedestrian crossing	—	*Odan hodo*	112
51	Counting	—	*Kazoe kata*	114
52	Finger Family	—	*Yubi kazoku*	116
53	Making a vow using your fingers	—	*Yubi kiri*	118
54	Please! / Sorry.	—	*Onegai! / Gomen.*	120
55	Grab this finger!	—	*Kono yubi tomare!*	122
56	Aren't I cute?	—	*Kawaii?*	124
57	You are so silly!	—	*Oshiri pen pen!*	126
58	Na-nana-na-na. Sticking out the tongue	—	Akkanbeee. *Shita wo dasu*	128
59	Rock-paper-scissors!	—	*Jan ken*	130
60	They're deeply in love!	—	*Achichi!*	132
61	Flower	—	*Hana*	134
62	Your underwear is showing	—	*Pan tsuu maru mie*	136
63	Stars shining brightly	—	*Ohoshisama kira kira*	138
64	Peace	—	*Piisu*	140
65	That's that!	—	*Engacho!*	142
66	Barrier!	—	*Bariaaah!*	144
67	Passing by a funeral car	—	*Reikyusha ga toru*	146
68	I'm angry	—	*Fukurettsura*	148
69	*Hooray!*	—	*Banzai!*	150
70	*Gatchohhhhn!*	—	*Gatchooooon!*	152

Something special for you
Golf 154

【日英対訳】日本人のしぐさ

70 Japanese Gestures

2015 年 5 月 9 日　初版第 1 刷発行

著　者	ハミル・アキ
発行者	浦　　晋　亮
発行所	IBCパブリッシング株式会社 〒162-0804 東京都新宿区中里町 29-3 菱秀神楽坂ビル 9F Tel. 03-3513-4511　Fax. 03-3513-4512 www.ibcpub.co.jp
印刷所	株式会社シナノパブリッシングプレス

© 2004 by Hamiru・aqui
© 2015 IBC Publishing, Inc.

落丁本・乱丁本は、小社宛にお送りください。送料小社負担にてお取り替えいたします。本書の無断複写(コピー)は著作権法上での例外を除き禁じられています。

Printed in Japan
ISBN978-4-7946-0343-2